Heart Healthy Mediterranean Diet Cookbook for Beginners

Heart Healthy Mediterranean Diet Cookbook for Beginners

+ 21 day meal plan and list products

BY VERONICA GARDENI

© Copyright 2023 Veronica Gardeni
All rights reserved.
No part of the contents of this book may be reproduced, duplicated by electronic or mechanical means transmitted without the direct written permission of the author or publisher.
In no event shall the publisher or the author be held legally responsible for any damage, compensation or monetary loss caused directly or indirectly by the information contained in this book.
Legal Notice:
This book is copyrighted and is intended for personal use only. You may not alter, distribute, sell, use, quote or paraphrase any part or content of this book without the author's permission.
Disclaimer Note:
Please note that the information contained in this document is for educational and entertainment purposes.
The content of this book is derived from various sources and the author's knowledge of the subject matter. Every effort has been made to present accurate, up-to-date, reliable and complete information.
No guarantees are declared or implied. Readers acknowledge that the author does not provide legal, financial, medical or professional advice. A licensed professional should be consulted before attempting any of the techniques presented in this book.
By reading this document, the reader accepts that the author is not liable for any damages, direct or indirect, incurred as a result of the use of the information contained in this document, including, but not limited to, inaccuracies.

TABLE OF CONTENTS:

INTRODUCTION 6
RECIPES FOR BREAKFAST 9
SCRAMBLED EGGS IN OLIVE OIL WITH
SUN-DRIED TOMATOES 9
TOASTED BREAD WITH MOZZARELLA
AND MUSHROOMS 11
PUMPKIN PIES 12
SANDWICH WITH HUMMUS,PICKLED CUCUMBER
AND TURKEY 13
SALAD OF FRESH SEASONAL FRUITS AND LEAFY GREENS
AND CHEESE 14
BARLEY GROATS WITH BANANA AND STRAWBERRIES 15
OATMEAL WITH RAISINS, NUTS AND APPLE 16
MACKEREL OR TUNA PASTE FOR SANDWICHES 17
PANCAKES WITH RICOTTA AND APPLES 18
STUFFED CHERRY TOMATOES WITH COTTAGE CHEESE 19
SCRAMBLED EGGS WITH GREEN BEANS AND CHIVES 20
BAKED BUNS WITH VEGETABLES AND EGG 21
CARROT BANANA AND STRAWBERRY PANCAKES 22
WHOLE WHEAT BREAD WITH SALMON AND OLIVES 23
COCONUT PANCAKES WITH RASPBERRIES 24
YOGURT WITH TANGERINE, BLUEBERRIES AND NUTS 25
CHICKEN MOZZARELLA AND TOMATO SALAD 26
SCRAMBLED EGGS WITH ASPARAGUS 2
PANCAKES WITH CHEESE 2
BANANA IN BATTER ....
TROUT PASTE SANDWICHES ....
RECIPES FOR LUNCH ....
ROASTED ZUCCHINI WITH SPICES ....
CREAM SOUP WITH RUTABAGAS AND CARROTS ....
PEPERONATA WITH HERBS ....

SPAGHETTI CARBONARA WITH HERBS 34
VEGETABLE STEW CAPONATA 35
RED BEAN CUTLETS WITH SOY SAUCE 36
PIZZA WITH SHRIMP AND HERBS 37
TOFU WITH VEGETABLES 38
CAULIFLOWER SOUP WITH ONIONS 39
ROASTED KOHLRABI WITH TOMATO SAUCE 40
BOTWINA COOLER SOUP 41
PASTA CASSEROLE WITH CHICKEN AND VEGETABLES 42
STEAMED FISH 43
CHICKEN WITH SPINACH 44
PASTA WITH SPINACH AND SALMON 45
LIGHT BEET SOUP 46
VEGETABLE PANCAKES 47
PUMPKIN SALAD 48
SHRIMP IN BUTTER WITH GARLIC AND THYME 49
BUCKWHEAT GROATS WITH EGG 50
ALAD WITH CRANBERRIES 51
CIPES FOR DINNER 52
DITERRANEAN CLASSIC SALAD 52
HO WITH MUSHROOMS AND ZUCCHINI 53
D SALMON WITH SPICES 54
D APPLES WITH CINNAMON 55
WITH OLIVES 56
ITH SPINACH 57
N RISOTTO WITH SPICES 58
AS IN TOMATO SAUCE 59
LET WITH LEEK AND MARJORAM 60
H BRAISED FENNEL AND ARUGULA 61
WITH KIMCHI AND MAPLE SYRUP 62
I WITH EGG AND SPICES 63
REAM SAUCE AND HERBS 65
SELS 66
H SUN-DRIED TOMATOES AND OLIVES 67
TUFFED ZUCCHINI 68

PASTA WITH NUTS AND CREAM SAUCE 69

OMELETTE WITH AVOCADO 70

POLENTA FRIES 71

PASTA SALAD WITH SALAMI AND SPICES 72

PASTA CASSEROLE WITH CHICKEN 73

RECIPES FOR DESSERTS 74

CHOCOLATE TART WITH STRAWBERRIES 74

DESSERT COTTA WITH STRAWBERRIES AND RASPBERRIES 76

COCKTAIL WITH KALE AND FRUIT 77

BLUEBERRY MUFFINS 78

PUMPKIN AND SUNFLOWER CAKE 79

DESSERT OF STRAWBERRIES AND MASCARPONE 80

GRILLED VEGETABLE SKEWERS 81

DESSERT WITH WATERMELON 82

FRIED BANANAS 83

OATCAKES 84

TART WITH CHERRIES 85

FLOURLESS PANCAKES WITH MAPLE SYRUP 86

RASPBERRY JAM 87

SUGAR-FREE BROWNIE 88

CHOCOLATE MOUSSE 89

VANILLA PUDDING WITH BANANA 90

BUCKWHEAT WITH COTTAGE CHEESE AND FRUIT 91

COUNTRY CHEESE AND RAISIN PANCAKES 92

TART WITH OREO AND CREAM 93

ZEPPOLE DOUGHNUTS WITH CREAM 94

ASIAN CHEESECAKE 95

SUMMARY TIPS AND CONCLUSION 96

28 DAYS MEAL PLAN 97

MEDITERRANEAN CUISINE AND DIET

Mediterranean cuisine , is a cuisine that is characterized by healthy and traditional cuisine from the Mediterranean area. This cuisine differs from all others primarily because of its amazing dishes. Typical ingredients are fish and seafood, various kinds of vegetables and fruits, olive oil used both for frying and as a dressing. Meat dishes play a secondary role, usually grilled or fried. Fruits vegetables natural oils and beverages that accompany meals.Among such drinks we can mention all kinds of natural fruit juices lemonades and healthy wine.

HOW TO TAKE CARE OF YOUR HEART THROUGH NUTRITION

Here are some rules to help you take care of your heart.

- Regular activity - healthy exercise walking jogging running
- Healthy eating - The best diet for the heart
- Good sleep essential and rest in the chat of the day
- A calm head without stress, a calm heart
- Alcohol either not at all or rarely in small amounts
- Quit smoking and other stimulants

- Vegetables - green vegetables broccoli, cauliflower, tomato, cucumber, kale, spinach, lettuces, carrots.
- Nuts and seeds - walnuts, macadamias, cashews, hazelnuts, almonds, sunflower seeds, pumpkin seeds.
- Legumes - lentils, beans, chick peas.
- Fruits - apple, citrus, pear, grapes, figs, melons, peaches, nectarines, dates.
- Herbs and spices - garlic, basil, oregano, rosemary, sage, mint, pepper.
- Fish and seafood - sea fish salmon, mackerel, sardines, tuna, freshwater fish, crabs, clams, oysters, shrimp.
- Whole grain products - brown rice, whole grain bread, mountain oatmeal, pasta.
- Meats - chicken, turkey, duck, occasional red meat.
- Zoonotic products - eggs, cheese, Greek yogurt.
- Fats - extra virgin olive oil, avocado, unrefined oils.

Experts describe the Mediterranean diet as the healthiest, as it has been scientifically proven to have many health benefits over, for example, the Western diet. A review of studies shows benefits in the form of:

- improved quality of life and well-being,
- reduced risk of heart attack and heart failure,
- reduced risk of stroke,
- improved cognitive function,
- reduced cancer risk,
- increased fitness

The Mediterranean diet has advantages such that the distribution of individual macronutrients (carbohydrates,protein, fats) depends on the type of diet. However, each of them contains a fairly large amount of healthy fats. Example distributions are the healthiest for the human body.

- 40% carbohydrates.
- 25% protein,
- 35% fats

The Mediterranean diet relies on certain dietary principles:what to limit and what to eat often.

Consume often:

- fresh vegetables and fruits,fish and seafood and rivers nuts, seeds, whole grains, herbs, legumes and, of course, lots of olive oil.
- Consume in moderation: poultry, dairy, eggs.
- Occasionally: red meat.fried meat with spicy additives
- Eliminate from your diet plan:

white flour products, cured meats (except homemade without artificial preservatives, sweetened beverages, sugary snacks, sugar, ready-made sauces, margarines, refined oils (including but not limited to: rapeseed, sunflower, palm) and any trans fats

The basis is to keep your body well hydrated - so remember to drink at least 1.5 2 liters of water a day. This amount will increase if you work physically or during hot days. It's a good idea to always have a bottle of water at hand and sip it in small sips.

A very important part of the Mediterranean diet is wines especially red wines . During this diet you can drink a glass of wine with lunch or dinner - although this is not required, of course. Red wines as well as white wine contain resveratrol - a substance considered to prolong life. This compound fights free radicals, reduces the risk of cardiovascular disease and promotes the maintenance of overall health.Any alcohol drunk in moderation is permissible for our body.

Now the most important thing that goes behind the Mediterranean diet is the price of all the ingredients that go into it:

The cost of the diet depends on what specific products are included.E.g. Shrimp, olives,or seafood salmon oysters are not among the cheapest. More frugal people can buy fish from local markets or from local fishermen catching fresh fish. Vegetables and fruits during the season it is worth buying from small farms, while in the off-season it is worth buying frozen mixtures.Vegetables can also be planted yourself spices sown if someone has a piece of land near the house.Natural own products are the best.

Also, all this information about the Mediterranean Diet will certainly come in handy for the rest of your life to get healthy and live a full healthy life.

In the rest of the book you will find plenty of recipes for breakfast lunch dinner afternoon snack for this miracle diet.

SCRAMBLED EGGS IN OLIVE OIL WITH SUN-DRIED TOMATOES

SERVINGS: 2 servings

COOKING TIME: 3-6 minutes

Ingredients:
4 large eggs
2 large raspberry tomato - 250 g
3 teaspoons of butter and 3 teaspoons of olive oil
spoonful of chives
a large pinch of salt and a smaller pinch of pepper

Energy per serving : 100 g
calorie count 150 kcal
Protein 10 g
Carbohydrates 2 g
Glycemic index 20

INSTRUCTIONS:

Crack four large eggs into a bowl. Using a whisk, make them into a smooth kogel mogel.

Wash and peel two large raspberry tomatoes weighing about 250 grams. You can also slit the tomato slightly. Then scald it with boiling water and remove the thin skin. If you have smaller tomatoes, use three or four pieces with a total weight of about 250 grams.

Cut the tomato into smaller pieces. In a small frying pan melt a teaspoon of butter and a tablespoon of olive oil.Add the chopped tomato and a tablespoon of chopped chives and a pinch each of salt and pepper. Fry the tomato sauce like this for five minutes on a low burner power. After this time, pour the whole thing into a bowl and wipe the pan dry.

Put the second teaspoon of butter and two tablespoons of olive oil in the pan and melt them on a low burner power. Pour in all the egg liquid. Stir the scrambled eggs all the time. The scrambled eggs should be perfect after about two minutes of stirring. At the end, lightly salt the scrambled eggs.

Scrambled eggs with tomatoes with this amount of ingredients is enough for two servings. Place the scrambled eggs on the plates first. In turn, on top of the scrambled eggs lay the tomato sauce. You can additionally sprinkle the whole thing with chives and sprinkle with freshly ground pepper.Also add basil.

Such Scrambled Eggs with tomatoes taste wonderful with a slice of fresh bread and orange juice.

TOASTED BREAD WITH MOZZARELLA AND MUSHROOMS

SERVINGS: 2 servings

COOKING TIME: 5-10 minutes

Ingredients:
toasted bread 4 slices
onion
1 piece mushroom
mozzarella balls 200 grams
black or white pepper
cherry tomatoes 1 teaspoon
garlic clove
pumpkin seeds
fine-grained iodized sea salt 1 teaspoon

INSTRUCTIONS:

Cut onions into smaller pieces and fry in butter.
Add sliced mushrooms to the onions and fry together for about 8 minutes,slice the mozzarella.
Wash tomatoes cut into pieces we can halve and add to mushrooms.
We also add pressed garlic and pepper and salt.
Toast bread in a sandwich form.
Put the mushroom stuffing - putting also a spoonful each of pumpkin seeds and sunflower seeds.
Bake the sandwiches and serve.

Energy per serving : 100 g
calorie count 100 kcal
Protein 7 g
Carbohydrates 5 g
Glycemic index 25

PUMPKIN PIES

SERVINGS: 2 servings

COOKING TIME: 15-20 minutes

Ingredients:
pumpkin 100 g
wheat flour 100 g
natural yogurt 50 g
medium eggs 2 pcs.
vanilla sugar 10 g
baking powder 3 g
olive oil 3 ml

INSTRUCTIONS:

Peel and grate the pumpkin so that you have a cup of grated pumpkin.
Mix yogurt with eggs then add pumpkin and mix all together.
Prepare flour with sugar and baking powder and mix together
To the pumpkin mixed with eggs yogurt add dry ingredients that is
flour mixed with baking powder sugar.
Mix the whole thing well slowly.
At the end let the dough stand for 10-15 minutes.
In a frying pan heat the oil, it can be canola oil or olive oil.
Scoop a spoonful of batter at a time and transfer it to the pan, making
pancakes.
Put the baked pancakes on a plate and enjoy a delicious breakfast

Energy per serving : 100 g
calorie count 185 kcal
Protein 6 g
Carbohydrates 16 g
Glycemic index 60

SANDWICH WITH HUMMUS,PICKLED CUCUMBER AND TURKEY

SERVINGS: 2 servings

COOKING TIME: 5 minutes

Ingredients:
Rye bread - two slice (70 g)
Turkey ham - 4 slices (100 g)
Natural hummus - 2 tablespoons (40 g)
white pepper - pinch

INSTRUCTIONS:

Spread the sandwich with hummus.
We put a slice of ham on the sandwich.
On the ham - sliced pickled cucumber.
Season to taste with a pinch of pepper
A tasty sandwich is ready.

Along with this delicious breakfast, you can drink a glass or two of delicious citrus juice

Energy per serving : 100 g
calorie count 220 kcal
Protein 18 g
Carbohydrates 28 g
Glycemic index 30

SALAD OF FRESH SEASONAL FRUITS AND LEAFY GREENS AND CHEESE

SERVINGS: 2 servings

COOKING TIME: 5 - 10 minutes

Ingredients:
25 g of goat hard cheese
100 g of fruit (e.g. strawberries, blueberries, raspberries,)
three handfuls of salad mix, e.g. a combination of arugula and iceberg
lettuce or lettuce with spinach and arugula
4 radishes
4 slices of Black Forest ham
thick balsamic sauce
7 slices of green cucumber
Olive oil
pepper , salt

INSTRUCTIONS:

Cut the fruit strawberries blueberries and others into 3 or 4 parts
depending on how big specimens you have. Then cut the radish and
cucumber into slices.
On the plate pour the salad mix, then add the fruit, cucumber and
radish. Shred the ham in your hands and arrange it on top of the
salad. Crumble the goat cheese with your hands and arrange on the
salad.
Then season the salad with pepper and salt. Finally, drizzle with olive
oil and balsamic dressing.

Energy per serving : 100 g
calorie count 185 kcal
Protein 10 g
Carbohydrates 6 g
Glycemic index 25

BARLEY GROATS WITH BANANA AND STRAWBERRIES

SERVINGS: 2 servings

COOKING TIME: 35 minutes

Ingredients:
1 cup of millet groats
2 bananas
2 tbsp almond flakes
2 cups of coconut or plant milk
100 g of fresh or frozen strasberries
2 tbsp honey

INSTRUCTIONS:

Rinse the semolina and add to the saucepan .
To the semolina add milk , cover and cook for about 25 - 30 minutes.
Watch that the semolina does not stick to the bottom .
Once cooked , transfer to a bowl , slice the bananas .
Blend until the consistency of pudding .
Add strawberries on top .
You can add nuts or almonds .
At the end pour with honey .

Energy per serving : 100 g
calorie count 125 kcal
Protein 8 g
Carbohydrates 25 g
Glycemic index 50

OATMEAL WITH RAISINS, NUTS AND APPLE

SERVINGS: 2 servings

COOKING TIME: 5 minutes

Ingredients:
6 tablespoons of mountain oatmeal
2 cups of milk
2 small apples
3 dried prunes
2 tablespoons of raisins
2 teaspoons honey
pinch of salt
a handful of walnuts or hazelnuts
pinch of cinnamon

INSTRUCTIONS:

Pour boiling water over prunes and raisins for a few minutes. Drain. Pour milk over oatmeal, add a pinch of salt.
When the water or milk boils, add the drained prunes and raisins. Cook the oatmeal for a few minutes, stirring frequently until it thickens noticeably.
Transfer to a bowl. Wash, peel and grate the apple. Add to oatmeal and stir. Sweeten the oatmeal with honey and sprinkle a handful of nuts.Such oatmeal with apple and nuts can be eaten warm for breakfast.

Energy per serving : 100 g
calorie count 100 kcal
Protein 3 g
Carbohydrates 20 g
Glycemic index 70

MACKEREL OR TUNA PASTE FOR SANDWICHES

SERVINGS: 2 servings

COOKING TIME: 10 - 20 minutes

Ingredients:
1 small smoked mackerel or 200gr can of tuna
2 hard boiled eggs
2 pickled cucumbers
2 tablespoons of mayonnaise
1 teaspoon of mustard
1 teaspoon horseradish
1 small red onion
pepper and salt

INSTRUCTIONS:

Hard boil the eggs, let them cool slightly, then peel them from their shells and chop them finely.
Separate the smoked mackerel, remove the backbone and spine.Then chop with a knife.
Pickled cucumbers and cut into small cubes and red onion very finely chopped.
Combine all the paste ingredients in a bowl. Add mayonnaise, mustard and horseradish.
Season the paste to taste with an ordobin of salt and pepper.
Decorate the top of the paste with chopped chives. Serve the smoked mackerel paste with bread.

Energy per serving : 100 g
calorie count 180 kcal
Protein 15 g
Carbohydrates 2 g
Glycemic index 20

PANCAKES WITH RICOTTA AND APPLES

SERVINGS: 2 servings

COOKING TIME: 10 - 20 minutes

Ingredients:
4 apples
2 eggs
300 g ricotta cheese
350 ml buttermilk
1 tsp sugar
1 teaspoon vanilla extract
150 g wheat flour
1 teaspoon baking powder
1/4 teaspoon baking soda
1/2 teaspoon cinnamon
7 tablespoons of butter
7 tablespoons of oil

INSTRUCTIONS:

Crack an egg into a bowl, give buttermilk, ricotta, sugar and vanilla extract and mix thoroughly.
Add flour, baking powder, baking soda, cinnamon and salt.Mix again until ingredients are combined.
Peel the apple and cut into slices.
In a frying pan, heat 3 tablespoons of butter and 3 tablespoons of oil.
Place 5 apple slices and fry for about a minute.
Pour 2 tablespoons of batter over each apple slice. Fry until bubbles appear on the surface of the pancakes. Then turn the pancakes to the other side and fry for about 2 more minutes.
Repeat with the remaining batter and apple slices.

Energy per serving : 100 g
calorie count 140 kcal
Protein 5 g
Carbohydrates 20 g, Glycemic index 65

STUFFED CHERRY TOMATOES WITH COTTAGE CHEESE

SERVINGS: 2 servings

COOKING TIME: 10 - 15 minutes

Ingredients:
half kg of cherry tomatoes
220 g semi-skimmed soft cottage cheese
1 red bell pepper
salt, pepper
2-4 tablespoons of chopped chives
3 Tbsp natural yogurt
sweet paprika

INSTRUCTIONS:

Cut off the bottom of the tomatoes minimally so that they stand on our plate.Cut off the top of the tomatoes.Using a tiny spoon, scrape the soft center out of the tomatoes and grate the cheese with 2 tablespoons of yogurt, ground bell pepper, salt and pepper.
Add the finely diced peppers. Then mix everything together,use a tiny spoon to spoon the cheese into the tomatoes.
Sprinkle with the remaining paprika and chopped chives. Arrange the caps on the tomatoes.

Energy per serving : 100 g
calorie count 125 kcal
Protein 8 g
Carbohydrates 7 g
Glycemic index 28

SCRAMBLED EGGS WITH GREEN BEANS AND CHIVES

SERVINGS: 2 servings

COOKING TIME: 10 - 15 minutes

Ingredients:

Half a package of 200 g of green beans whole already prepared by steaming

40 g smoked bacon

25 g butter

5 eggs

Salt and pepper

INSTRUCTIONS:

Slice bacon and fry with butter.

When it browns, add the beans and fry together for about 5 minutes.

Slide the beans with the bacon to the side of the pan.

On the free part, we break the eggs. Gently stir the whites without breaking the yolks yet.

When the egg whites are almost set, stir the whole thing and season to taste with salt and pepper. After a while, we remove from the heat.

Energy per serving : 100 g

calorie count 135 kcal

Protein 8 g

Carbohydrates 3 g

Glycemic index 40

BAKED BUNS WITH VEGETABLES AND EGG

SERVINGS: 2 servings

COOKING TIME: 25 minutes

Ingredients:
200 g Black Beans
100 g red bell pepper
80 g grated yellow cheese
4 Kaiser rolls or small buns
4 eggs
1 onion
Pepper and salt
oregano

INSTRUCTIONS:

We cut the top of the buns.Press the flesh to the bottom,forming bowls.
Preheat the oven to 375°F heat the buns for 5 minutes about , during
this time cut finely onions and peppers.
Drain the beans from the marinade and rinse them.Season with salt
and pepper.
Fill the baked buns with vegetables and crack one egg into each.
Bake the buns for about 15 minutes or until the eggs are set.
After removing from the oven, sprinkle with chopped chives and
oregano.

Energy per serving : 100 g
calorie count 155 kcal
Protein 10 g
Carbohydrates 3 g
Glycemic index 35

CARROT BANANA AND STRAWBERRY PANCAKES

SERVINGS: 2 servings

COOKING TIME: 15 minutes

Ingredients:
Can of carrots about 200 ml
2 tablespoons of fine sugar
2 teaspoons powdered sugar
1 egg
50 g wheat flour
2 tbsp oil
2 tbsp milk
8 strawberries
2 bananas
half a teaspoon of cinnamon
half a teaspoon of baking powder

INSTRUCTIONS:

Drain carrots, peel bananas slice strawberries and egg into a container, blitz to a smooth paste.Add milk, sugar, flour, baking powder,cinnamon. Blend until all ingredients are combined.In a frying pan heat oil.
Apply small portions of batter, fry on medium heat for a few minutes on each side, until the pancakes are browned.
Transfer the pancakes to a plate, sprinkle with powdered sugar.

Energy per serving : 100 g
calorie count 100 kcal
Protein 8 g
Carbohydrates 11 g
Glycemic index 45

WHOLE WHEAT BREAD WITH SALMON AND OLIVES

SERVINGS: 2 servings

COOKING TIME: 5 minutes

Ingredients:
4 slices of whole wheat bread,
60g smoked salmon,
6g dark or green olives
pinch of oregano
pinch of pepper

INSTRUCTIONS:

Spread 4 slices of whole wheat bread lightly with butter.
Put slices of smoked salmon on it
Cut the olives into striped slices,put them on the bread
Finally, sprinkle oregano to taste and you can add a pinch of pepper

For such a breakfast you can also make a delicious salad of tomato
with garlic olive oil and lemon juice.This is a wonderful composition for
bread with salmon.

Ideal to drink for such a breakfast is grape juice

Energy per serving : 100 g
calorie count 250 kcal
Protein 15 g
Carbohydrates 11 g
Glycemic index 70

COCONUT PANCAKES WITH RASPBERRIES

SERVINGS: 2 servings

COOKING TIME: 5 - 15 minutes

Ingredients:
3 eggs
Half a teaspoon of coconut oil
3 teaspoons of coconut flour
2 tablespoons of maple syrup
Raspberries
Cinnamon

INSTRUCTIONS:

Prepare eggs mix them with flour and cinnamon.
Heat coconut oil in a pan and pour the batter over the pancakes.
Fry them like this until they are browned on all sides.
Pour maple syrup over the finished pancakes and eat with sliced raspberries.
In addition, you can sip them with forest fruit juice for this delicious breakfast.
The perfect form of a good healthy breakfast

Energy per serving : 100 g
calorie count 300 kcal
Protein 14 g
Carbohydrates 28 g
Glycemic index 35

YOGURT WITH TANGERINE, BLUEBERRIES AND NUTS

SERVINGS: 2 servings

COOKING TIME: 5 minutes

Ingredients:
300 g - 2 packs of natural yogurt
handful of walnuts or hazelnuts
4 handfuls of blueberries
2 mandarins

INSTRUCTIONS:

Peel the mandarins from the peel and cut into cubes.
Finely chop the nuts on a tray.
Add all the ingredients together.
Mix everything with yogurt.
In addition, you can sprinkle with cinnamon.

Energy per serving : 100 g
calorie count 330 kcal
Protein 14 g
Carbohydrates 30 g
Glycemic index 60

CHICKEN MOZZARELLA AND TOMATO SALAD

SERVINGS: 2 servings

COOKING TIME: 15 minutes

Ingredients:
100g smoked chicken
half a ball of mozzarella
2 tomatoes
spoon of shelled sunflower seeds
spoon of linseed oil or olive oil
Two handfuls of lettuce
chives
salt, pepper to taste

INSTRUCTIONS:

Cut the chicken into cubes.
We also dice the tomato mozzarella into small pieces.
We add lettuce, chopped chives.
Finally, linseed oil or olive oil.
We season everything with salt pepper herbs and mix.

We recommend apple or grape juice made from ripe fruit for this
delicious breakfast.

Energy per serving : 100 g
calorie count 160 kcal
Protein 9 g
Carbohydrates 3 g
Glycemic index 25

SCRAMBLED EGGS WITH ASPARAGUS

SERVINGS: 2 servings

COOKING TIME: 15 minutes

Ingredients:
6 green asparagus
4 eggs
salt
pepper
chives
olive oil

INSTRUCTIONS:

Rinse the asparagus under running water.
Cut into small pieces.
We pour olive oil in a frying pan
We sauté the asparagus for about 5 minutes.
We break the eggs into a bowl. Season with salt and pepper.
Scramble the spiced eggs with a fork and pour them into the pan with
the fried asparagus.
Mix everything together. Serve with crusty bread or toast.

Energy per serving : 100 g
calorie count 135 kcal
Protein 8 g
Carbohydrates 3 g
Glycemic index 40

PANCAKES WITH CHEESE

SERVINGS: 2 servings

COOKING TIME: 15 minutes

Ingredients for the dough :
200 g 1 and 1/3 cup of whole wheat flour
3 eggs
glass of warm water
half a glass of warm milk
50 g 1/4 cube of melted butter
spoonful of sugar

Ingredients for cheese for pancakes:
500 g semi-skimmed ground cottage cheese
30 g - 2 tablespoons of 18% sour cream 30 g
Vanilla sugar
1 egg yolk

INSTRUCTIONS:

Add egg yolk, sugar, vanilla sugar, two tablespoons of sour cream to cottage cheese and mix In a bowl pour flour, beat eggs.
Pour in a cup of warm water and half a cup of warm milk. To this we add another tablespoon of fine sugar, we mix the whole thing.Finally, we pour in the butter. We continue to mix the pancake batter for a while more, set aside for 10 minutes to rest. We heat up the frying pan. Stir the batter , pour enough batter into the pan so that the mixture freely covers the surface of the pan. After a minute or so, flip the pancake to the other side. In this way we fry all the pancakes. We fill the pancakes with stuffing, which we fry in clarified butter before serving.

Energy per serving : 100 g
calorie count 130 kcal
Protein 9 g
Carbohydrates 13 g , Glycemic index 75

BANANA IN BATTER

SERVINGS: 2 servings

COOKING TIME: 25 minutes

Ingredients:
4 bananas
2 eggs
80 g sour cream
1/4 teaspoon of baking soda
100 g whole wheat flour
oil for frying
pinch of salt

INSTRUCTIONS:

Heat a frying pan with oil.
Cut the banana into thin slices about 0.5 cm thick.
In a bowl, whisk the egg with the cream, add a pinch of salt and baking soda. Add whole wheat flour in batches, stirring constantly to make a smooth batter.
Dip the banana slices into the batter, preferably with a fork, to coat them on all sides.
Fry the banana in a skillet, about 1-2 minutes on each side or until browned and crispy.
Serve with toppings, such as honey natural yogurt, maple syrup, jam or peanut butter and fruit.

Energy per serving : 100 g
calorie count 200 kcal
Protein 4 g
Carbohydrates 24 g
Glycemic index 70

TROUT PASTE SANDWICHES

SERVINGS: 2 servings

COOKING TIME: 30 minutes

Ingredients:
Half of a smoked trout
250 g feta cheese,or other cottage cheese
50 g of your favorite mayonnaise
1 shallot onion
20 g chopped sun-dried tomatoes
1 bunch of fresh dill
pinch of sea salt
pinch of freshly ground pepper
bread to serve

INSTRUCTIONS:

Peel the fish from the bones and skin. Place the pieces in a bowl.
Add crumbled feta cheese or other cottage cheese. Cut the sun-dried
tomatoes into very small cubes. Add mayonnaise or yogurt if you
prefer a lighter version.
Mash everything with a fork or blitz to a smooth paste. Season with
spices.In the meantime, chop dill or chives finely. Add to the paste and
mix everything gently.
Garnish the paste with fresh dill and serve on toast or crusty fresh
bread.You can season the trout paste with horseradish.

Energy per serving : 100 g
calorie count 140 kcal
Protein 8 g
Carbohydrates 13 g
Glycemic index 50

ROASTED ZUCCHINI WITH SPICES

SERVINGS: 2 servings

COOKING TIME: 20-30 minutes

Ingredients:
500 g zucchini
20 ml olive oil
30 g Parmesan or other cheese
60 g almonds
Salt and pepper 2 pinches
chives
oregano

INSTRUCTIONS:

Preheat the oven to 450°F
Cut zucchini into slices about 3-5 mm.thick
In a bowl mix grated cheese,ground almonds breadcrumbs and
oregano and pepper.
Sprinkle zucchini with sea salt, brush with olive oil, coat with sprinkles,
place in an ovenproof mold or on a baking sheet and place in the
oven.
Bake for about 20 minutes until golden brown. Serve with sour cream
or ketchup, fresh thyme and chives.

Energy per serving : 100 g
calorie count 105 kcal
Protein 5 g
Carbohydrates 5 g
Glycemic index 65

CREAM SOUP WITH RUTABAGAS AND CARROTS

SERVINGS: 2 - 4 servings

COOKING TIME: 20-30 minutes

Ingredients:
500 g Brussels sprouts
100 g Carrots
400 ml Vegetable bouillon with a stock cube
Milk 3.2% 100 ml
100 g Onion
100 g Light bread
30 ml Canola oil or sunflower oil
1 g Fresh bear garlic
Salt pepper herbes de Provence nutmeg

INSTRUCTIONS:

Peel Brussels sprouts carrots and onions.
Wash the vegetables thoroughly. Divide the Brussels sprouts in half, dice the carrots and onions.
In a pot or high pan, heat the oil, then fry the onion in it. When it glazes, add carrots and Brussels sprouts.
Fry for a few minutes, stirring briefly every now and then.
Pour in the broth, add salt, pepper and a teaspoon of garlic bear herbes de Provence.

Energy per serving : 100 g
calorie count 50 kcal
Protein 2 g
Carbohydrates 8 g
Glycemic index 36

PEPERONATA WITH HERBS

SERVINGS: 2 servings

COOKING TIME: 15 minutes

Ingredients:
150 g red peppers
150 g green peppers
100 g Yellow peppers
250 g Tomato
25 ml rapeseed oil
15 g Medium garlic
75 g Young onion
15 ml Wine vinegar
13 g Parsley
salt black and white pepper
herbs de Provence

INSTRUCTIONS:

Clean the peppers from the seed nests. Cut them into larger cubes.
Finely dice the onion and garlic.
Cut the tomatoes into cubes.
In a frying pan, heat the oil, fry the onion and garlic, and finally add the tomatoes. Season with salt, pepper and oregano. Simmer for 5 minutes.
Add the peppers, pour in the wine vinegar and simmer another 10 minutes.
Finally, sprinkle with parsley and herbs de Provence.

Energy per serving : 100 g
calorie count 60 kcal
Protein 1 g
Carbohydrates 8 g
Glycemic index 39

SPAGHETTI CARBONARA WITH HERBS

SERVINGS: 2 servings

COOKING TIME: 15 - 20 minutes

Ingredients:
170 g dark or light semolina pasta
140 g smoked bacon
4 eggs
70 g yellow parmesan cheese
Salt, pepper, oregano, minced garlic
herbes de Provence

INSTRUCTIONS:

Cook pasta 5-7 minutes as per instructions.
Crack eggs into a bowl and season with pepper and salt.
Mix firmly thoroughly.
In a skillet, fry the finely chopped bacon to brown slightly.
Add 3/4 of the cheese to the egg mixture and mix well.The whole thing then season with garlic and herbs.
Add the pasta to the pan to the bacon and stir decently, heat all the time.
Finally, slowly pour in the sauce, stirring all the time.
The sauce should be light creamy and the eggs should not curdle.
Serve the finished pasta sprinkled with Parmesan cheese and herbs de Provence and pepper.

Energy per serving : 100 g
calorie count 330 kcal
Protein 22 g
Carbohydrates 24 g
Glycemic index 57

VEGETABLE STEW CAPONATA

SERVINGS: 2 servings

COOKING TIME: 20-40 minutes

Ingredients:
350 g eggplant
50 g celery
250 g red bell bell pepper
50 g pickled green olives
60 g onion
20 g capers
150 g canned tomatoes
15 ml olive oil
20 g raisins
20 g pine nuts
20 ml olive oil
Wine vinegar
salt pepper basil parsley oregano

INSTRUCTIONS:

Cut eggplants into cubes, marinate with salt and set aside for 30 minutes.
Rinse the eggplants and fry them in hot oil.
Remove from the pan, fry diced peppers, onions and celery in the same pan.
Add raisins, capers, canned tomatoes olives and eggplant at the end.
Simmer until the vegetables are tender, season with vinegar, hot bell pepper and basil with salt and pepper. Sprinkle the caponata at the end with parsley and pine nuts and oregano.

Energy per serving : 100 g
calorie count 30 kcal
Protein 2 g
Carbohydrates 7 g
Glycemic index 40

RED BEAN CUTLETS WITH SOY SAUCE

SERVINGS: 2 servings

COOKING TIME: 20 minutes

Ingredients:
150 g red beans
1 pc small egg
20 g breadcrumbs
10 ml rapeseed or sunflower oil
pinch of salt and pepper
hot bell pepper
soy sauce

INSTRUCTIONS:

Prepare the beans and drain them.
Blend to a smooth paste.
Add egg, bread crumbs, and season with half a teaspoon of hot bell
pepper and salt and pepper.
Mix thoroughly and form cutlets.
Heat the oil and fry in a pan.
At the end, season the cutlets and pour a little soy sauce over them.

The dish pairs perfectly with cooked couscous, and for sipping, cherry
and apple juice is the perfect beverage.

Energy per serving : 100 g
calorie count 350 kcal
Protein 20 g
Carbohydrates 50 g
Glycemic index 70

PIZZA WITH SHRIMP AND HERBS

SERVINGS: 4 servings

COOKING TIME: 45 minutes

Ingredients:

150 g wheat flour   250 g mozzarella cheese

2 g salt   120 g spinach

10 g yeast   400 g Tomatoes

15 ml rapeseed or sunflower oil   lemon juice

Salt, pepper,oregano,marjoram

400 g shrimp

INSTRUCTIONS:

Before you prepare the dough defrost the shrimp, cut them open season them as desired.

Then prepare the dough ,dissolve fresh yeast in slightly warm water. Then mix thoroughly with flour,oil and salt.

You need to stretch the risen dough all over the pan and puncture it with a fork.

Then set aside for about 15 minutes to rise.

Spread the finished dough with tomato puree, top with shrimp and halved tomatoes.

Sprinkle the whole thing with grated mozzarella cheese. You can also add other cheese.

Bake in the oven for about 15 minutes at 450°F.

After removing the pizza from the oven, top with spinach and sprinkle with oregano and marjoram herbs.

Energy per serving : 100 g

calorie count 115 kcal

Protein 12 g

Carbohydrates 11 g

Glycemic index 42

TOFU WITH VEGETABLES

SERVINGS: 2 servings

COOKING TIME: 30 minutes

Ingredients:
400 g tofu
240 g red peppers
350 g zucchini
200 g yellow bell pepper
2 pieces carrots
2 cloves garlic
10 g ginger root
6 spoons soy sauce
bell pepper, sweet paprika, fresh chili bell pepper, parsley

INSTRUCTIONS:

Cut vegetables into strips,then chop ginger and garlic.
Dice the tofu and fry it in a pan with a small amount of
amount of oil.
Fry the garlic and ginger in the pan, then add the vegetables and tofu.
Sauté until the vegetables are softened.
Finally, add soy sauce and stir.
It is best to serve the dish with rice

Energy per serving : 100 g
calorie count 55 kcal
Protein 3.5 g
Carbohydrates 5.5 g
Glycemic index 40

CAULIFLOWER SOUP WITH ONIONS

SERVINGS: 2 servings

COOKING TIME: 30 minutes

Ingredients:
500 g Cauliflower
100 g carrots
200 g new potatoes
700 ml vegetable bouillon
5 g 18% cream
20 g dill
5 g butter
20 g onion
salt, pepper,
marjoram, allspice

INSTRUCTIONS:

Cut the potatoes into cubes.
Cut cauliflower into smaller pieces to that carrots cut.
Finely chop the onion,and in the meantime in a pot melt
and heat the butter.
Throw in the onion and sauté until browned.
Add the rest of the vegetables and sauté over low heat covered for
about 5 - 8 minutes.
At the end pour broth over the whole thing.Season with spices.
Cook covered until all vegetables are soft.
Put the cream into a glass.
In a glass with cream pour gradually 2 tablespoons of hot soup.
Stir and pour such cream into the pot.
Add chopped dill, season with herbs.

Energy per serving : 100 g
calorie count 28 kcal
Protein 1.5 g
Carbohydrates 4 g , Glycemic index 40

ROASTED KOHLRABI WITH TOMATO SAUCE

SERVINGS: 4 servings

COOKING TIME: 35 minutes

Ingredients:
500 g kohlrabi
60 ml olive oil
salt, pepper, a pinch to taste
thyme, basil,
minced garlic
tomato sauce
ketchup

INSTRUCTIONS:

Peel and slice the kohlrabi into thin strips.
In a bowl, mix the olive oil with herbs and seasonings.
Put kohlrabi in the bowl and mix thoroughly.
Line an oven tray with baking paper, spread the fritters on it.
Bake them in an oven preheated to 390 F for 30 minutes.
At the end, pour tomato sauce or ketchup over them

An ideal accompaniment to such kohlrabi fritters can also be
mayonnaise soy sauce or tartar sauce.
Recommended for this dish is a compote of strawberries and
elderberries or with red wine.

Energy per serving : 100 g
calorie count 100 kcal
Protein 1.5 g
Carbohydrates 6 g
Glycemic index 70

BOTWINA COOLER SOUP

SERVINGS: 4 servings

COOKING TIME: 15 minutes

Ingredients:
400 ml natural yogurt
300 g kefir
300 g botvin
200 g cucumber
3 eggs
150 g Radish
20 g Dill
240 g Cooked beets
pepper,salt,oregano

INSTRUCTIONS:

Prepare all vegetables and wash thoroughly.
Chop the beet, beets, cucumber and radishes into small cubes.
Hard boil the eggs for about 6 minutes.
Cut the dill with a knife into small pieces.
Put all the vegetables in a bowl and pour over yogurt and kefir.
Season to taste with salt and pepper.
Put in the refrigerator for 0.30 - 1 hour.
Serve such a soup with eggs and season with oregano.

Energy per serving : 100 g
calorie count 100 kcal
Protein 1.5 g
Carbohydrates 5.5 g
Glycemic index 45

PASTA CASSEROLE WITH CHICKEN AND VEGETABLES

SERVINGS: 4 servings

COOKING TIME: 25 minutes

Ingredients:
350 g penne pasta
220 g spinach
120 g mushrooms
150 ml Natural or Greek yogurt
0.5 cup green peas
200 gr chicken breast
1.5 pcs onion
125 g mozzarella or other cheese
4 tbsp olive oil
pepper and salt, herbs de Provence, oregano, marjoram

INSTRUCTIONS:

Cook the pasta al dente according to the instructions.
Heat 3 tablespoons of oil in a skillet and toss in the onion.
Add diced chicken, season with pepper and salt and red bell pepper.
Fry for 5 minutes. Later add the spinach , wait for a while.
Prepare a baking dish (heatproof) cover with a tablespoon of olive
oil. Later arrange the cooked pasta.
On a layer of pasta grate mushrooms and lay out peas.
Next, add the contents of the pan to the dish and mix everything.
In a bowl give natural yogurt with pepper, salt, herbs .
Pour the prepared sauce over the casserole.
At the very end grate mozzarella or other cheese.
Bake the whole thing in an oven preheated to 350 F for 15 minutes.

Energy per serving : 100 g
calorie count 130 kcal
Protein 8 g
Carbohydrates 10 g , Glycemic index 47

STEAMED FISH

SERVINGS: 2 servings

COOKING TIME: 25 minutes

Ingredients:
300 g cod fillet or pollock
30 ml olive oil
pepper,salt,
ginger
herbs de Provence
marjoram
lemon

INSTRUCTIONS:

Boil water in a steaming pot.
Peel the ginger root and cut into thin strips.
Rinse the fish fillets, dry them and place them in the steaming pot.
Sprinkle the fish fillets with pepper.
Then coat them with ginger.
Finally, close the lid of the steaming pot and cook the fish for about 10 minutes.
Serve the fish topped with olive oil and a squeeze of lemon juice.

A white lavender beer or dry red wine goes perfectly with such a composed dish.

Energy per serving : 100 g
calorie count 140 kcal
Protein 14 g
Carbohydrates 0 g
Glycemic index 40

CHICKEN WITH SPINACH

SERVINGS: 2 servings

COOKING TIME: 25 minutes

Ingredients:
200 g Skinless chicken breasts
100 g Spinach
36% Creamy cream
pepper,salt
garlic , oregano
marjoram

INSTRUCTIONS:

Prepare the chicken, coat it with oil,then in garlic and spices.
Fry in a pan for a few minutes.
Add the spinach to the pan with the chicken.
Fry until the spinach is slightly wilted.
Add cream and grated mozzarella or iny cheese.
At the end, mix everything thoroughly and season.
Serve the chicken with pasta or grits tastes best
For this dish the ideal drink composition will be a refreshing drink of
fresh fruit with mint.

Energy per serving : 100 g
calorie count 175 kcal
Protein 12 g
Carbohydrates 5 g
Glycemic index 20

PASTA WITH SPINACH AND SALMON

SERVINGS: 2 servings

COOKING TIME: 15 minutes

Ingredients:
200 g spaghetti noodles
180 g smoked salmon
70 g spinach
30% cream cheese
30 ml olive oil
10 g garlic
pepper and salt
garlic,oregano

INSTRUCTIONS:

Cook spaghetti pasta according to the instructions on the package,
al dente.
Cut the smoked salmon into pieces.
Later, in a frying pan, heat the oil. Fry the crushed garlic and fresh
spinach in it until the spinach starts to wilt.
Then pour the cream into the pan and bring to a boil.
Once it begins to boil, add the salmon.
Bring to a boil again, add the pasta and mix it all well.
Season with salt and pepper and oregano.
Finally, sprinkle with lemon juice to taste.
You can also add chives to garnish the dish.

Energy per serving : 100 g
calorie count 190 kcal
Protein 14 g
Carbohydrates 20 g
Glycemic index 38

LIGHT BEET SOUP

SERVINGS: 4 servings

COOKING TIME: 40 minutes

Ingredients:
400 g beets
800 ml vegetable bouillon
350 g potatoes
50 g onion
10 g garlic
10 g butter
100 g cream 18%
pepper,salt
allspice, bay leaf
marjoram

INSTRUCTIONS:

Peel and finely dice the beets and potatoes.
Finely chop the onion into bite-sized pieces.
Melt butter in a pot, add onions and fry everything.
Pour broth into the pot and heat until boiling.
Add the vegetables and boil again .
Later add two cloves of garlic, reduce the heat and cook covered for
about 25 minutes
until the vegetables are soft.
Add spices and tempered cream.
At the end, mix everything well.

Energy per serving : 100 g
calorie count 40 kcal
Protein 1 g
Carbohydrates 7 g
Glycemic index 70

VEGETABLE PANCAKES

SERVINGS: 4 servings

COOKING TIME: 30 minutes

Ingredients:
250 g zucchini
80 g onion
80 g carrot
150 g potatoes
3 eggs
60 g wheat flour
30 ml rapeseed oil
pepper,salt,turmeric

INSTRUCTIONS:

Peel carrots,onions,potatoes.
Grate zucchini with the rest of the vegetables.
Season with salt and pepper and leave for 12 minutes.
After this time, drain off the excess juice.
Later, add flour and eggs to the vegetables.
Mix everything thoroughly.
In a frying pan, heat the oil.
And put on the pan,pancakes and fry on both sides until golden brown.
They taste perfect with tomato sauce.

Energy per serving : 100 g
calorie count 120 kcal
Protein 5 g
Carbohydrates 14 g
Glycemic index 60

PUMPKIN SALAD

SERVINGS: 2 servings

COOKING TIME: 35 minutes

Ingredients:
50 g Feta cheese
200 g pumpkin
50 ml olive oil
2 tbsp honey
3 pcs fresh figs
1 tbsp lemon juice
1 tbsp Apple cider vinegar
half a handful arugula
small pomegranate, pepper,salt

INSTRUCTIONS:

Cut the pumpkin into slices.
On a baking sheet, mix pumpkin, a tablespoon of olive oil, honey, and
a pinch of salt and thyme.
Place in the oven and bake for 20 minutes.
After 20 minutes, remove from the oven, add the figs and mix all
together.
Return to the oven and bake for another 15 minutes, until the figs are
browned caramelized.
Later, in a bowl, mix the remaining olive oil, apple cider vinegar, lemon
juice, herbs de Provence, as well as pepper and a pinch of salt.
Put arugula in a large bowl and sprinkle roasted pumpkin with
figs.Finally, crumble feta on top and add pomegranate seeds on top.

Energy per serving : 100 g
calorie count 115 kcal
Protein 2 g
Carbohydrates 12 g
Glycemic index 20

SHRIMP IN BUTTER WITH GARLIC AND THYME

SERVINGS: 4 servings

COOKING TIME: 15 minutes

Ingredients:
400 g fresh or frozen shrimps
200 ml dry wine preferably white light
15 g garlic
60 g butter
20 g parsley
Thyme
salt , pepper

INSTRUCTIONS:

Prepare shrimp or thaw if you have frozen ones.
Peel the garlic and cut into thin slices.
Melt butter in a frying pan and fry the sliced garlic in it.
Add the shrimp to the pan
Season them with a pinch of salt and pepper.
Fry the whole thing for 3 minutes approximately.
After this time, pour wine into the pan and simmer until half of the
wine has evaporated.
Later, chop the parsley.
Serve the finished shrimp sprinkled with parsley and thyme.

Energy per serving : 100 g
calorie count 140 kcal
Protein 14 g
Carbohydrates 2 g
Glycemic index 30

BUCKWHEAT GROATS WITH EGG

SERVINGS: 2 servings

COOKING TIME: 25 minutes

Ingredients:
200 g buckwheat groats
1 pc small onion
10 g garlic
3 pcs. eggs
200 g red bell pepper
20 ml olive oil
300 g zucchini
Pepper,salt, garlic, herbes de Provence

INSTRUCTIONS:

Cook the semolina.
Peel and chop the onion and garlic.
Wash peppers, remove the seed nest and cut into cubes.
Dice the zucchini as well.
Heat oil in a frying pan and add garlic and onion.
Stir-fry for a while until glazed.
Add the peppers and zucchini. Stir-fry for a few minutes.
Add cooked semolina to the pan and stir. Season with salt and pepper
and sauté another 5-7 minutes.
Spread the semolina with the vegetables evenly in the pan. Make 3
indentations in it and crack eggs into them.
Cover the pan with a lid and heat until the eggs are set.
Finally, spread the finished porridge with eggs on plates and sprinkle
with herbes de Provence and green parsley.

Energy per serving : 100 g
calorie count 138 kcal
Protein 6 g
Carbohydrates 19 g
Glycemic index 65

SALAD WITH CRANBERRIES

SERVINGS: 2 servings

COOKING TIME: 20 minutes

Ingredients:
400 g smoked chicken breast fillet
250 g spinach
125 g gouda cheese
2 pcs pear
3 tbsp olive oil
80 g dried cranberries

INSTRUCTIONS:

First, cut the chicken breast into thin strips. Put the meat pieces in a bowl.
Rinse the spinach leaves and add to the meat.
Wash the pears and cut them into very thin slices. Add them to the rest of the salad ingredients.
Then add the cranberries to the salad bowl.
Mix all the ingredients thoroughly.In a bowl mix the oil of spices and herbs. Add a little powdered sugar. Mix the sauce vigorously and pour it over the salad.

Energy per serving : 100 g
calorie count 150 kcal
Protein 6 g
Carbohydrates 10 g
Glycemic index 48

MEDITERRANEAN CLASSIC SALAD

SERVINGS: 2 servings

COOKING TIME: 20 minutes

Ingredients:
250g Chicken Breasts
200 g romaine lettuce
4 slices bread
4 tbsp parmesan cheese
3 tbsp Mayonnaise
2 tbsp olive oil
parsley
pepper,salt, minced garlic

INSTRUCTIONS:

Cut the chicken breasts into smaller pieces,
Then rub it with olive oil, and sprinkle it with salt and pepper,put it on a heated pan and grill it.
When the meat is browned cool it and cut it into large cubes. Then transfer to a large bowl.
Wash the lettuce and add it to the bowl with the chicken.
Cut the bread into small cubes and fry it in a hot pan.
When the croutons are browned add to the rest of the salad ingredients.
In a bowl mix mayonnaise,chopped parsley, salt, pepper and garlic.Pour the prepared dressing over the salad, then mix everything together very thoroughly and sprinkle with grated Parmesan cheese.

Energy per serving : 100 g
calorie count 200 kcal
Protein 8 g
Carbohydrates 13 g
Glycemic index 65

LECHO WITH MUSHROOMS AND ZUCCHINI

SERVINGS: 2 servings

COOKING TIME: 25 minutes

Ingredients:
200 g zucchini
200 g mushrooms
200 g red peppers
200 g yellow peppers
300 g fresh or canned tomatoes
100 g onion
pepper,salt
herbs de Provence
basil,marjoram

INSTRUCTIONS:

At first, wash the mushrooms well, peel and cut them into small slices.
Then chop the onion finely,and
zucchini and peppers cut into larger slices.
In a frying pan, heat the oil, add the onions and sauté for a few
minutes.
Add the vegetables and mushrooms .
Season to taste with herbs and spices and sauté.
All then pour in tomatoes and simmer covered on medium heat.
A perfect dish that tastes good with rice.

Energy per serving : 100 g
calorie count 28 kcal
Protein 1.5 g
Carbohydrates 6 g
Glycemic index 15

BAKED SALMON WITH SPICES

SERVINGS: 2 servings

COOKING TIME: 30 minutes

Ingredients:
400 g salmon fillet
2 slices of lemon
2 tablespoons lemon juice
2 teaspoons butter
1 tbsp olive oil
20 g dill
pepper,salt
herbs de Provence
marjoram

INSTRUCTIONS:

Put the salmon on a piece of aluminum foil.Next to the salmon put
chopped dill.
Leave some of it and shred it.
Later, pour lemon juice over the salmon, put butter and olive oil on it.
Sprinkle a generous pinch of salt and pepper.
Place lemon slices on top of the salmon.
Thoroughly and tightly wrap in aluminum foil.
Bake in the oven for 20 minutes at 350°F.
An ideal dish that tastes good with red wine.

Energy per serving : 100 g
calorie count 260 kcal
Protein 14 g
Carbohydrates 5 g
Glycemic index 60

BAKED APPLES WITH CINNAMON

SERVINGS: 2 servings

COOKING TIME: 30 minutes

Ingredients:
300 g apple
30 g plum jam
60 g walnuts
30 g cashew nuts
Cinnamon

INSTRUCTIONS:

Wash the apples and cut off the top part
Using a teaspoon, hollow out the seed nests.
Put a portion of jam into the cavity,you can also use jam.
Cover the apple with the previously cut part and wrap it in aluminum
foil.
So that everything is tight.
Place in an oven preheated to 375°F for about 20-25 minutes.
Remove apples from oven and serve with nuts.

Energy per serving : 100 g
calorie count 70 kcal
Protein 1 g
Carbohydrates 18 g
Glycemic index 65

SALAD WITH OLIVES

SERVINGS: 2 servings

COOKING TIME: 10 minutes

Ingredients:
4 tomatoes
1 small onion
3 slices of ciabatta roll
3 tbsp olive oil
3 tbsp parmesan or other cheese
10 pcs green olives
pepper,salt,
oregano,marjoram

INSTRUCTIONS:

Slice ciabatta and toast in a pan.
Wash and slice the tomatoes ,put them in a bowl.
Add the olives to the tomatoes.
Chop the onion very finely and add to the tomatoes.
Mix olive oil with parmesan cheese,
Add a pinch of pepper and salt to taste, as well as marjoram and
oregano.
Thoroughly mix the entire salad.
Finally, tear the slices toasted in the pan into pieces and add to the
salad.

Energy per serving : 100 g
calorie count 100 kcal
Protein 3 g
Carbohydrates 7 g
Glycemic index 55

RICE WITH SPINACH

SERVINGS: 2 servings

COOKING TIME: 20 minutes

Ingredients:
200 g white rice
0.5 ml olive or canola oil
200g fresh or frozen spinach
pepper,salt,
arugula

INSTRUCTIONS:

To begin, pour oil in a pan and heat.
Add fresh or frozen spinach and fry until it separates.
Later, pour in the rinsed rice and fry together for a while.
Pour 3 cups of water into the pans.
Season the whole thing with pepper and salt.
Finally, cook covered for 15-20 minutes,
until the rice absorbs all the water.
Sprinkle everything with arugula.

Energy per serving : 100 g
calorie count 185 kcal
Protein 5 g
Carbohydrates 38 g
Glycemic index 75

PUMPKIN RISOTTO WITH SPICES

SERVINGS: 2 servings

COOKING TIME: 30 minutes

Ingredients:
100 g rice for risotto
5 tbsp olive oil
20 g shallot onion
100 g pumpkin
300 ml vegetable or broth bouillon
10 g butter
10 g Parmesan or other cheese
pepper, salt, marjoram

INSTRUCTIONS:

In a frying pan, heat the oil.
Add chopped onions.Dice the pumpkin add it to the onions in the pan and leave half for later.
Fry the whole thing quickly and add a small pinch of marjoram and a pinch of salt and pepper.Add the rice and fry until the rice turns shiny and slightly translucent. Place the pans over the lowest possible heat.
Add 1 ladle of warm broth and stir Leave until the rice absorbs the broth.
When a portion of the broth is absorbed by the rice, add another portion, stir and leave until the rice absorbs a portion.
Repeat like this all the time until the last portion of broth is absorbed.
Later, add the remaining portion of pumpkin.
Add butter and Parmesan cheese, season with salt and pepper to taste. At the end, mix thoroughly.

Energy per serving : 100 g
calorie count 100 kcal
Protein 2.5 g
Carbohydrates 15 g, Glycemic index 67

CHICKPEAS IN TOMATO SAUCE

SERVINGS: 2 servings

COOKING TIME: 30 minutes

Ingredients:
250 g chickpeas can be canned
20 g garlic
150 g Onion
150 g Tomatoes
20 ml canola oil
salt pepper
fresh ginger
cilantro,chili bell pepper,

INSTRUCTIONS:

Blend chili peppers garlic, and ginger.
Heat oil in a frying pan, then add chopped onions and fry for about 3-5 minutes.
Later as the onions brown add the garlic paste and fry about 3 minutes stirring occasionally.
Add, cilantro, pepper and continue to fry.
Later add tomatoes and simmer the whole thing over medium heat, about 5 minutes.
Add chickpeas and 0.5 cup of water. Again simmer the whole thing over low heat for a few minutes.
Season the chickpeas with salt and cilantro at the end.

Energy per serving : 100 g
calorie count 115 kcal
Protein 4 g
Carbohydrates 14 g
Glycemic index 55

TROUT FILLET WITH LEEK AND MARJORAM

SERVINGS: 2 servings

COOKING TIME: 30 minutes

Ingredients:
100 g fresh trout
1 tbsp olive oil
100 g leek
pepper, salt
marjoram
2 slices of sourdough rye bread

INSTRUCTIONS:

Wash and dry the trout fillet.
Season with salt, marjoram and pepper.
Then cut the leek into slices. We arrange the fish and leek on a piece
of baking paper.
Wrap tightly in the shape of a candy.
We put in an oven preheated to 375 F.
Bake for about 20-25 minutes.
Serve with rye bread drizzled with olive oil.
Of beverages to such a dish goes perfectly with red wine,or fresh
cherry juice.

Energy per serving : 100 g
calorie count 160 kcal
Protein 14 g
Carbohydrates 2 g
Glycemic index 50

PASTA WITH BRAISED FENNEL AND ARUGULA

SERVINGS: 2 servings

COOKING TIME: 30 minutes

Ingredients:
2 tbsp olive oil
200g fennel
3 tbsp whole wheat pasta -.
3 tbsp parmesan or other
parsley
salt, black pepper
Arugula handful

INSTRUCTIONS:

Cut fennel into thin slices.
In oil, fry the vegetable.
After a few minutes, pour a quarter cup of water and simmer covered
until the water evaporates.
If the dill will be hard, you can add more liquid and simmer it a few
minutes longer.Further season with Parmesan cheese, pepper, salt and
parsley and arugula.
Cook all dente whole grain pasta.
And serve with the pasta.
It goes perfectly with white or red wine.

Energy per serving : 100 g
calorie count 160 kcal
Protein 8 g
Carbohydrates 16 g
Glycemic index 48

PANCAKES WITH KIMCHI AND MAPLE SYRUP

SERVINGS: 2 servings

COOKING TIME: 15 minutes

Ingredients:
150 g kimchi
50 g spring onions
50 g wheat flour
50 g rice flour
4 tbsp sugar
3 eggs
40 ml canola oil
5 tbsp maple syrup

INSTRUCTIONS:

Chop the kimchi and onion finely.
Crack the eggs into a bowl, pour in the kimchi juice,
Later add both flours and sugar and mix.
Add kimchi and onions and mix thoroughly.
In a frying pan, heat the oil.
Now the batter must be applied in portions to the fat.
Fry on both sides until golden brown.
Serve the pancakes with soy sauce, water, a teaspoon of rice vinegar
and sugar and sesame seeds.
Finally, pour maple syrup on top.

Energy per serving : 100 g
calorie count 190 kcal
Protein 8 g
Carbohydrates 22 g
Glycemic index 40

KHACHAPURI WITH EGG AND SPICES

SERVINGS: 2 servings

COOKING TIME: 60 minutes

Ingredients:
500 g wheat flour type 500
3.2% 200 ml milk
25 g Fresh yeast
5 g sugar
5 g salt
200 g cottage cheese
50 g mozzarella cheese
50 g Feta cheese
4 tbsp 30% cream cheese
4 tbsp olive oil
100 g g gouda or other yellow cheese
4 eggs
1 tbsp honey
Garlic
pepper,salt

INSTRUCTIONS: STEP 1

Prepare a bowl and pour warm milk into it.
Later add crushed yeast, sugar and 2 tablespoons of flour.
Mix thoroughly and set aside to rise.
Once the dough has risen, add the remaining flour,
150 ml of water, salt and oil.
Knead the dough until it is smooth and springy.
Cover the bowl with a cloth and set aside in a warm place for an hour.

INSTRUCTIONS: STEP 2

In the meantime, prepare the filling: in another bowl, mix the crushed cottage cheese with cream.
Add honey and salt and pepper to taste and pressed garlic.
Grate the mozzarella and add the fetta cheese crumbled into small pieces.
Add to the stuffing and mix thoroughly.
Divide the risen dough into 4 equal parts.
Roll out each part gently.
Form into boats, curling the edges slightly inward.
Later grate the yellow cheese and sprinkle the bottom of the previously formed boats.
Arrange a thick layer of the prepared stuffing on top.
Bake the chachapuri for about 15 - 20 minutes at 395 deg. F.
After this time, take them out of the oven.
Then crack an egg onto each chachapuri.
Bake for about 10 more minutes, so that the yolk is still liquid.
Serve warm.
This dish is perfect with fresh juices or compote.

Energy per serving : 100 g
calorie count 330 kcal
Protein 12 g
Carbohydrates 36 g
Glycemic index 90

SHRIMP IN CREAM SAUCE AND HERBS

SERVINGS: 2 servings

COOKING TIME: 25 minutes

Ingredients:
200 g 30% cream cheese
300 g shrimp
20 g butter
50 ml white wine, preferably dry
5 g garlic
2 pcs chilli peppers
10 g lemon
parsley
pepper,salt, parsley,garlic, herbs de Provence

INSTRUCTIONS:

Clean the shrimp and dry with a towel.
Finely chop the chili peppers and grate the garlic.
Heat the pan well and melt butter or olive oil in it.
Add the garlic and chilies to the pan. Sauté for a while.
Add the shrimp and fry them briefly on both sides until they are lightly browned.
Pour in the wine and fry together until it gently evaporates.
Later, add the cream and season with salt and pepper and simmer together until the cream evaporates a little.
Chop the parsley and add it to the pan.
At the very end, sprinkle the whole thing with lemon juice.
Serve with white or red wine.

Energy per serving : 100 g
calorie count 150 kcal
Protein 13 g
Carbohydrates 1.5 g , Glycemic index 15

BRAISED MUSSELS

SERVINGS: 2 servings

COOKING TIME: 15 minutes

Ingredients:
400 g mussels
120 ml dry or semi-dry white wine
50 g butter
2 tbsp olive oil
garlic,salt,
parsley

INSTRUCTIONS:

Wash the clams,not closed discard them.
In a pot melt butter and fry 2 chopped garlic cloves on it.
Then add wine and clams.
Simmer on low heat for about 5 minutes, until the clams open.
Later, chop half a bunch of parsley and add it to the stewed mussels.
Shake the pot to mix the clams with the parsley and butter-wine sauce.
Eat the clams open.
They taste perfect with vegetables and wine.

Energy per serving : 100 g
calorie count 90 kcal
Protein 4.5 g
Carbohydrates 2.5 g
Glycemic index 15

FOCACCIA WITH SUN-DRIED TOMATOES AND OLIVES

SERVINGS: 2 servings

COOKING TIME: 60 minutes

Ingredients:
350 g wheat flour
1 teaspoon salt
200 ml water
2 teaspoons sugar
2 tbsp olive oil
10 g fresh yeast
15 pcs. Green and black olives
4 slices sun-dried tomatoes from oil
1 tsp coarse salt, oregano,marjoram

INSTRUCTIONS:

Dissolve yeast in warm water and let stand for 5 - 7 minutes. Then mix with flour, oil and salt.
We knead the dough and set aside in a warm place for an hour to rise.
We cover the dish in which we keep the dough with a cotton cloth.
After an hour, we transfer the dough to a baking tray and make indentations with our fingers. It is best to grease your hands with olive oil.
We put sliced olives and sun-dried tomatoes on the dough and sprinkle the whole thing with coarse salt.
We set aside for another half an hour.
Bake at 425 F for 25 minutes. The dough should brown.
It tastes perfect dipped in olive oil and sprinkled with oregano or marjoram.

Energy per serving : 100 g
calorie count 360 kcal
Protein 46 g
Carbohydrates 10 g , Glycemic index 70

GREEK-STYLE STUFFED ZUCCHINI

SERVINGS: 2 servings

COOKING TIME: 30 minutes

Ingredients:
2 medium zucchini
1/2 red bell pepper
1/2 cup of dry millet groats
2 tomatoes
Light or dark olives
Mozzarella cheese and feta cheese
3 cloves of garlic
Oregano
Basil, Marjoram, Salt and pepper

INSTRUCTIONS:

At the beginning we cook the porridge.
We wash the zucchini and take out the center.
We season with pepper and salt.
We put it in a preheated oven for 5-8 minutes or on the grill, and roast
it to soften a little.
Put the cooked millet groats into a bowl and add chopped dark
olives,feta cheese, tomato, red bell pepper, pressed garlic, oregano,
basil, marjoram and pepper.
Mix everything, then put it on the hollowed out zucchini and sprinkle
with grated mozzarella cheese.
Bake about 10- 15 minutes in the oven or on the grill in wrapped
aluminum foil.

Energy per serving : 100 g
calorie count 73 kcal
Protein 4 g
Carbohydrates 4 g , Glycemic index 40

PASTA WITH NUTS AND CREAM SAUCE

SERVINGS: 2 servings

COOKING TIME: 40 minutes

Ingredients:
3 tablespoons of whole wheat flour
1 cup 18% cream
300 g chocolate macaroni
2-3 tbsp sugar
pinch of vanilla sugar
3 handfuls of nuts nuts raisins pistachios etc.
3 tbsp honey
1 tbsp coconut oil

INSTRUCTIONS:

Boil the pasta and drain.
Mix flour and half a cup of water into a smooth paste. Heat another
half cup of water and add cream mix and boil.
Add flour with water to the boiling cream.
Pour while stirring so as not to leave lumps, boil. Remove from heat
and add vanilla sugar to taste and mix all together.
Gently crush nuts such as nuts
In a pan melt coconut oil, add honey and nuts.
Fry the whole thing for a while, stirring.
Finally, put the pasta on a plate, pour the cream sauce over it and top
with the nuts.
Ideally this dish tastes with fresh juices or red wine.

Energy per serving : 100 g
calorie count 260 kcal
Protein 6 g
Carbohydrates 28 g , Glycemic index 65

OMELETTE WITH AVOCADO

SERVINGS: 2 servings

COOKING TIME: 15 minutes

Ingredients:
3 eggs
1/2 avocado
2 tablespoons of milk
8 olives
40 g feta cheese
chives
Small onion
Turmeric
Canola oil or butter
Pepper and salt

INSTRUCTIONS:

Peel and chop the onion and avocado into small cubes,
We discard the seeds from the avocado.
We crumble feta cheese into small pieces.
Chop the chives and olives
Crack the eggs into a bowl, add the milk and salt and whisk the
mixture for a while to make air bubbles,pepper and turmeric add.
Fry the onion in a pan preheated.
Pour the mixture of beaten eggs into the pan and fry for about 2-3
minutes.
Then add avocado, feta cheese , olives and sprinkle with chives.
Season everything to taste with spices.
Fry everything until the omelet is completely crusted.

Energy per serving : 100 g
calorie count 125 kcal
Protein 6 g
Carbohydrates 3 g , Glycemic index 50

POLENTA FRIES

SERVINGS: 2 servings

COOKING TIME: 25 minutes

Ingredients:
120 g polenta semolina or corn porridge
2 cups water
salt, chili
pepper, parsley,
oregano,
200 ml 12-18% cream
olive oil for baking

INSTRUCTIONS:

It is best to use instant porridge for this recipe.
Slowly pour it over salted boiling water.
With the instant version it will take a few minutes.
Later add the rest of the additives, parsley, salt, chili. Further add,
cheese, pepper.
Further we put the mixture on baking paper, after cooling cut into
shapes of fries. They are placed on lightly sprinkled baking paper and
baked for 10 -12 minutes on each of two sides.
Serve them with a sauce previously prepared with cream and parsley
and sprinkle with oregano.
They also taste perfect with tomato sauce.

Energy per serving : 100 g
calorie count 120 kcal
Protein 4 g
Carbohydrates 6 g
Glycemic index 30

PASTA SALAD WITH SALAMI AND SPICES

SERVINGS: 2 servings

COOKING TIME: 20 minutes

Ingredients:
100g pasta,bow-tie or shells
50 g salami
3 slices cherry tomatoes or regular tomatoes
4 slices sun-dried tomatoes
10 pcs black or green olives
50 g canned corn
2 tbsp flaxseed
2 tbsp oil from under the sun-dried tomatoes
pinch sugar
herbes de Provence
Pepper,salt

INSTRUCTIONS:

Cook the pasta according to the instructions on the package. Drain
and add corn, sun-dried tomatoes and olives.
Later add sliced tomatoes.
Cut salami into cubes or slices, add to the salad.
Later, combine the ingredients for the dressing.Mix with the salad.
Put the salad in the refrigerator - chill, it is best cold.
Sprinkle with flaxseed and marjoram.

Energy per serving : 100 g
calorie count 180 kcal
Protein 8 g
Carbohydrates 28 g
Glycemic index 75

PASTA CASSEROLE WITH CHICKEN

SERVINGS: 4 servings

COOKING TIME: 25 minutes

Ingredients:
350 g penne pasta
150 g spinach
100 g mushrooms
150 ml 0% Greek yogurt
1 piece onion
50 g green peas
125 g mozzarella cheese
3 spoons olive oil 50 ml
Pepper,salt,herbes de Provence,marjoram

INSTRUCTIONS:

Cook the pasta.
Slice the onion then heat 2 tablespoons of oil in a pan and add the onion and diced chicken, season with salt and pepper.
Fry for a few minutes 5-10 minutes. Add the spinach and fry for a few minutes.
Coat an ovenproof dish with 1 tablespoon of olive oil.
Arrange cooked pasta on the bottom.On this pasta grate mushrooms and layer peas. Next add the contents of the pan to the dish.
Mix everything together with a spoon.
In a bowl mix natural yogurt with pepper, salt, herbs.Pour the finished sauce over the casserole.
Grate mozzarella on top.
Bake the whole thing in an oven preheated to 375 F for 15 minutes.

Energy per serving : 100 g
calorie count 155 kcal
Protein 7 g
Carbohydrates 16 g , Glycemic index 65

CHOCOLATE TART WITH STRAWBERRIES

SERVINGS: 4 servings

COOKING TIME: 50 minutes

Ingredients:
150 g wheat flour type 500
40 g cocoa powder
40 g sugar
150 g butter
4 pcs egg yolks
10 ml vanilla extract
150 g dark chocolate
200 g 30% cream cheese
350 g strawberries
20 g powdered sugar

INSTRUCTIONS: STEP 1

Sift flour together with cocoa into a bowl.
Cut the butter (150 g) into small cubes and add it to the bowl along with the sugar.
Later, you need to mix to form a crumble consistency and all the ingredients combine.
Add a teaspoon of vanilla extract and egg yolks, knead the whole thing thoroughly.
Finally, wrap the dough in plastic wrap and place in the refrigerator for 25 minutes.

INSTRUCTIONS: STEP 2

Take the chilled dough out of the refrigerator, roll it out
and spread it on a tart pan.
Cover the top with baking paper and put something over it.
Bake for 15 - 20 minutes at 395 F.
After this time, pull off the paper and bake for another 5 minutes.
Once it's baked leave it to cool.
Continue pouring the cream and 2 teaspoons of vanilla extract into a
saucepan. Heat, but do not bring to a boil.
Prepare the chocolate and break it into smaller pieces and add it to
the saucepan. Stir until the chocolate melts.
Add a tablespoon of butter and stir.
Arrange some of the strawberries on the cooled bottom and pour the
warm chocolate cream over them.
Put the tart in the refrigerator for at least 20 minutes.
Before serving on the table, arrange the remaining strawberries on top
and dust with powdered sugar.

Energy per serving : 100 g
calorie count 370 kcal
Protein 5.5 g
Carbohydrates 30 g
Glycemic index 80

DESSERT COTTA WITH STRAWBERRIES AND RASPBERRIES

SERVINGS: 2 servings

COOKING TIME: 25 minutes

Ingredients:
10 g gelatin
125 ml 36% cream cheese
125 ml 2% milk
10 g powdered sugar
120 g raspberries and strawberries
vanilla sugar

INSTRUCTIONS:

Prepare 3 tablespoons of warm water in a bowl and add the gelatin.
Mix thoroughly and set aside for 10-15 minutes.
Pour cream and milk into a pot, add powdered sugar and vanilla
sugar. Stir and boil, when boiling remove from gas burner.
Add gelatin to the pot and mix thoroughly.Later, pour the whole thing
into 4 dishes and refrigerate for 3 hours to chill.
In a pot heat raspberries and strawberries with a little powdered
sugar,add a little water and simmer for 10 minutes.
Pour such a mousse over the finished dessert.

Energy per serving : 100 g
calorie count 215 kcal
Protein 3.8 g
Carbohydrates 8.8 g
Glycemic index 65

COCKTAIL WITH KALE AND FRUIT

SERVINGS: 2 servings

COOKING TIME: 10 minutes

Ingredients:
2 pieces banana
200 g kale
3 pieces pear
2 pieces Kiwi
20 g ginger root
Lemon or lime juice

INSTRUCTIONS:

At first, peel the fruit from the skins,then
slice and transfer to a tall dish,
add kale leaves,a little lemon juice and ginger.
Finally, add 1 liter of water preferably spring water.
Blend everything later until smooth.
Pour into glasses.

Energy per serving : 100 g
calorie count 170 kcal
Protein 1.1 g
Carbohydrates 14 g
Glycemic index 45

BLUEBERRY MUFFINS

SERVINGS: 4 servings

COOKING TIME: 30 minutes

Ingredients:
100 g Wheat flour type 500
50 g sugar
10 g vanilla sugar
100 ml 3.2% milk
36 ml canola oil
5 g baking powder
1 pc egg
100 g blueberries
salt,baking powder

INSTRUCTIONS:

Pour flour into a bowl, then add sugar and vanilla sugar,then baking
powder and a small pinch of salt. Mix thoroughly a few times.
In another bowl of a dish, beat eggs, pour milk and oil and mix
thoroughly.
Pour the wet ingredients into the dry ones. Mix.
Add blueberries and gently mix again.
Pour the batter into muffin tins.
Bake for 20 minutes at 420 F.

Energy per serving : 100 g
calorie count 270 kcal
Protein 5 g
Carbohydrates 35 g
Glycemic index 85

PUMPKIN AND SUNFLOWER CAKE

SERVINGS: 4 servings

COOKING TIME: 60 minutes

Ingredients:
100 g of sunflower seed puree
100 g pumpkin puree
100 g banana
80 ml 2% milk
80 g whole wheat flour
2 g baking soda
1 g baking powder
2 g cinnamon

INSTRUCTIONS:

Put pumpkin puree and sunflower puree , peeled banana and pour
milk into a bowl.
Blend to a smooth paste.
Then add flour, baking soda, baking powder and cinnamon to the
bowl. Mix the whole mixture.
Pour the dry ingredients into the wet ones and mix thoroughly.
Line a fruitcake pan with baking paper. Pour the batter into the mold.
Bake for 40-45 minutes at 350 F. To a dry stick.

Energy per serving : 100 g
calorie count 150 kcal
Protein 5,5 g
Carbohydrates 34 g
Glycemic index 60

DESSERT OF STRAWBERRIES AND MASCARPONE

SERVINGS: 4 servings

COOKING TIME: 15 minutes

Ingredients:
300 g strawberries
300 g Strawberries
10 g sugar
200 g mascarpone
10 g powdered sugar
150 g 30% cream cheese
100 g sponge cake

INSTRUCTIONS:

Wash and dry the strawberries and Strawberries. Remove the stalks from them.
Place strawberries strawberries and sugar in the blender cup. Blend the whole thing to a smooth paste.
Whip the cream until stiff with the addition of powdered sugar.
Add the mascarpone to the cream and blend the whole to a smooth cream.
In a goblet or cup, place the strawberry and strawberry mixture. On top of this pour the cream with mascarpone.In addition, for dessert give sponge cakes with fresh strawberries and strawberries.

Energy per serving : 180 g
calorie count 135 kcal
Protein 2,5 g
Carbohydrates 18 g
Glycemic index 85

GRILLED VEGETABLE SKEWERS

SERVINGS: 2 servings

COOKING TIME: 35 minutes

Ingredients:
200 g red peppers
200 g yellow peppers
200 g Zucchini
200 g eggplant
160 g marinated mushrooms
20 ml Olive oil
oregano a pinch
sweet paprika a pinch
marjoram pinch

INSTRUCTIONS:

Wash and slice the vegetables.
Wash and peel mushrooms too , cut into thin slices.
Coat vegetables in oil and spices solidly.
You need to stuff the slices of vegetables and mushrooms alternately
on wooden skewer sticks.
Grill the skewers for about 12-18 minutes, checking every now and then
and turning to the other side so that they do not burn.
Wheat beer or red wine is ideal for this dish.

Energy per serving : 100 g
calorie count 50 kcal
Protein 1,2 g
Carbohydrates 4.8 g
Glycemic index 15

DESSERT WITH WATERMELON

SERVINGS: 4 servings

COOKING TIME: 30 minutes

Ingredients:
200 ml of natural yogurt
2 teaspoons chia seeds
2 teaspoons sugar
2 watermelon jellies each for 500 ml of water
pieces of fresh watermelon

INSTRUCTIONS:

Boil the jellies in 1l of water.
Later prepare yogurt sweeten it and add chia seeds. Set aside in the
refrigerator overnight for swelling.
Place the yogurt, prepared in this way, on the bottom of goblets or
glasses of dishes.On top of it, put the thickening jelly and raw
watermelon.
Place the desserts in the refrigerator, chilling them well.

Energy per serving : 100 g
calorie count 200 kcal
Protein 3,0 g
Carbohydrates 4.5 g
Glycemic index 40

FRIED BANANAS

SERVINGS: 2 servings

COOKING TIME: 15 minutes

Ingredients:
240 g bananas
20 g maple syrup
10 g cinnamon
10 g butter

INSTRUCTIONS:

Peel the banana from the skin and cut it lengthwise in half.
Heat the pan well and fry the sliced banana on both sides for a few
minutes.
While frying, sprinkle with cinnamon.
Finally, put the finished banana on a plate and pour maple
syrup over it.
It also tastes perfect topped with red wine.

Energy per serving : 100 g
calorie count 130 kcal
Protein 1,0 g
Carbohydrates 27 g
Glycemic index 52

OATCAKES

SERVINGS: 4 servings

COOKING TIME: 35 minutes

Ingredients:
70 g butter
140 g Oatmeal
40 g Dessert chocolate
20 g Sunflower seeds
10 g powdered sugar
30 g gluten-free whole grain oat flour
1 pc egg
5 g baking powder

INSTRUCTIONS:

Heat a frying pan and melt the butter.
Put oatmeal, flour, sunflower seeds vanilla powdered sugar and baking powder into a large dish such as a bowl. Whisk in the eggs and grate the chocolate. Add melted butter and mix well.
Form small, flat cookies from the oat mixture.
Arrange them on a baking paper-lined oven tray.
Bake the whole thing in an oven preheated to 350 degrees for 20 - 25 minutes.
They taste perfect with fresh juice.

Energy per serving : 100 g
calorie count 280 kcal
Protein 10 g
Carbohydrates 38 g
Glycemic index 55

TART WITH CHERRIES

SERVINGS: 8 servings

COOKING TIME: 60 minutes

Ingredients:
220 g wheat flour type 500
10 g potato flour
60 g sugar
120 g butter
1 piece. Egg
400 g Cherries
Vanilla sugar
baking powder

INSTRUCTIONS:

Put 150 g of flour, 100 g of cold, diced butter, an egg, 0.5 teaspoon of baking powder, 0.5 packet of vanilla sugar and 60 g of sugar into a large bowl and knead to form a smooth dough.
Secure the dough with plastic wrap and store in the refrigerator.
Wash the cherries, stone them and cut them into halves.
Mix the fruit with the starch.
Then preheat the oven to 180 degrees C.
Grease the mold thinly with oil.
Roll out the cooled dough to put it in the mold.
Prick with a fork in several places and bake for 15 minutes approximately.
Knead 100 g of flour, 50 g of cold butter, 50 g of sugar and 0.5 packet of sugar with vanilla sugar and make a crumble, then set aside in the refrigerator.On the baked bottom put the fruit.
Sprinkle the top of the cake with crumble.
Bake the cake for 35 minutes.

Energy per serving : 100 g
calorie count 290 kcal
Protein 4.4 g,Carbohydrates 34 g ,Glycemic index 90

FLOURLESS PANCAKES WITH MAPLE SYRUP

SERVINGS: 2 servings

COOKING TIME: 40 minutes

Ingredients:
130 g semolina
1 pc egg
250 ml milk 1.5%
15 ml rapeseed oil
pinch of stevia

INSTRUCTIONS:

First, pour the semolina into a bowl, then pour in the milk.
Mix the whole thing thoroughly and set the bowl aside for about 20-30 minutes.
After 30 minutes, beat an egg, pour in a little oil and add stevia sweetener, if necessary.
Mix everything thoroughly.
Later, pour a portion of the batter on the heated oil and fry the pancakes on both sides until golden brown.

Energy per serving : 100 g
calorie count 180 kcal
Protein 7 g
Carbohydrates 24 g
Glycemic index 52

RASPBERRY JAM

SERVINGS: 4 servings

COOKING TIME: 40 minutes

Ingredients:
500 g raspberries
50 g sugar or sweetener

INSTRUCTIONS:

Pour 200 ml of water into a pot.Bring to a boil and add sugar.
Stir thoroughly until the sugar dissolves.
Rinse the raspberries in a strainer and add them to the boiling water.
Later, give a small fire under the pot.
Gently stir everything.
Cook for about 35-40 minutes.
In the meantime, do not stir the contents, but gently shake the pot
slightly.
You can pour the finished jam into clean jars, or dishes that can be
tightly sealed.

Energy per serving : 100 g
calorie count 110 kcal
Protein 1 g
Carbohydrates 26 g
Glycemic index 80

SUGAR-FREE BROWNIE

SERVINGS: 4 servings

COOKING TIME: 50 minutes

Ingredients:
50 dried prunes
50 g dried dates
170 g canned chickpeas
50 g Peanut (groundnut) butter
330 g cocoa powder

INSTRUCTIONS:

Pour hot water over prunes and dates and leave for 15-20 minutes.
Prepare a large bowl dish and place chickpeas,peanut butter, cocoa
and drained dates and prunes.
Then blend everything to a smooth paste.
Finally, pour into a baking pan lined with baking paper.
Bake for 30-35 minutes at 350 F.

Energy per serving : 100 g
calorie count 230 kcal
Protein 9 g
Carbohydrates 35 g
Glycemic index 70

CHOCOLATE MOUSSE

SERVINGS: 4 servings

COOKING TIME: 50 minutes

Ingredients:
2 cups granulated erythritol or other low-carb sweetener
4 tsps. vanilla extract
4 cups sugar-free chocolate chips, melted
4 cups heavy cream
4 tbsps. gelatin powdered
1/4 cups cold water

INSTRUCTIONS:

In a large mixer bowl, beat stiff cream, erythritol and vanilla extract until stiff.
In a separate bowl, mix the melted chocolate and powdered gelatin. Add cold water and mix well
Later, gently stir the chocolate into the whipped cream until completely combined.
Divide the mousse into 4 individual goblets or transfer to a large serving dish.
Chill the mousse in the refrigerator for at least 1.5 to 2 hours or until set.
Serve chilled with chocolate chips sprinkled on top and berries.

Energy per serving : 100 g
calorie count 180 kcal
Protein 7 g
Carbohydrates 20 g
Glycemic index 65

VANILLA PUDDING WITH BANANA

SERVINGS: 2 servings

COOKING TIME: 25 minutes

Ingredients:
400 ml 2% milk
150 g banana
40 g potato flour
2/3 teaspoon vanilla extract
Sweetener such as erythritol

INSTRUCTIONS:

Prepare a peeled banana and blitz it with 300 ml of milk and vanilla extract.
Pour into a pot and bring to a boil.
Meanwhile, mix in the remaining 100 ml of milk with potato flour.
Later pour the flour with the milk into the pot.
Cook over low heat, stirring constantly, until the pudding thickens

Energy per serving : 100 g
calorie count 85 kcal
Protein 3 g
Carbohydrates 14 g
Glycemic index 80

BUCKWHEAT WITH COTTAGE CHEESE AND FRUIT

SERVINGS: 2 servings

COOKING TIME: 20 minutes

Ingredients:
100 g buckwheat flakes
100 g of skim cottage cheese
150 g strawberries
100 g american strawberries
50 g blueberries
20 g coconut shavings

INSTRUCTIONS:

Wash the fruit and peel off the leaves.
Later, we pour boiling water over the flakes with half of the coconut
shavings and set aside to swell.
Add the rest of the ingredients on top and sprinkle with coconut
shavings.

Energy per serving : 100 g
calorie count 100 kcal
Protein 5 g
Carbohydrates 11 g
Glycemic index 65

COUNTRY CHEESE AND RAISIN PANCAKES

SERVINGS: 4 servings

COOKING TIME: 20 minutes

Ingredients:
1 egg
1.5 cups flour
country cheese 200 g
1 tablespoon sugar
0.5 teaspoon soda
0.5 teaspoon baking powder
handful of raisins
Vanilla sugar
oil for frying

INSTRUCTIONS:

Crack an egg into a bowl, add vanilla sugar and sugar, then beat until fluffy.
Then add country cheese and sifted flour with baking powder and baking soda.
Mix everything thoroughly add raisins. Set aside for 5 minutes.In a frying pan heat oil, spoon small portions of batter and fry on low heat until golden brown on both sides.
Remove to a paper towel to drain from excess fat.Sprinkle the pancakes with powdered sugar.
You can serve with your favorite toppings such as whipped cream with maple syrup or chocolate sauce.

Energy per serving : 100 g
calorie count 220 kcal
Protein 8 g
Carbohydrates 18 g , Glycemic index 82

TART WITH OREO AND CREAM

SERVINGS: 4 servings

COOKING TIME: 45 minutes

Ingredients:
200 g oreo cookie
50 g butter
250 g mascarpone
50 g white chocolate
200 g raspberries
2 tbsp coconut shavings

INSTRUCTIONS:

Crumble the Oreo cookies and grind them in a food processor together with the butter.
Put the resulting mixture into a baking pan and knead to form the bottom for the tart.
Place in the refrigerator for about 25-40 minutes.
Melt white chocolate in a water bath and mix with mascarpone.
Spread the chocolate mixture over the oreo bottom.
Sprinkle coconut shavings on top and arrange raspberries.

Energy per serving : 100 g
calorie count 320 kcal
Protein 3 g
Carbohydrates 22 g
Glycemic index 75

ZEPPOLE DOUGHNUTS WITH CREAM

SERVINGS: 4 servings

COOKING TIME: 60 minutes

Ingredients:
150 g wheat flour
125 g sugar
3 eggs
175 g butter
500 ml 3.2% milk
100 g Cherry or raspberry jam
3 pcs egg yolks
Coconut shavings

INSTRUCTIONS:

Place 150 g of butter and 320 ml of water in a pot and heat until it melts.
Later remove from heat and add 250 g of whole wheat flour and mix. Let the batter cool and beat the eggs into it.
Add a pinch of salt and mix until fluffy.Continue to put the dough into a pastry sleeve. Then on the baking paper squeeze the dough from the sleeve into doughnuts.
Bake in a preheated 375F degrees for 20 minutes.
In a saucepan, place egg yolks, sugar and 50 g of whole wheat flour. Stir to combine ingredients.Pour in milk and simmer for 10 minutes. Let the mixture cool all the way down.
To this mixture add 200 g of butter and sugar with vanilla and mix to a smooth cream. Stuff cooled doughnuts with cream on top sprinkle with powdered sugar and give cherry jam.

Energy per serving : 100 g
calorie count 250 kcal
Protein 5.5 g
Carbohydrates 23 g , Glycemic index 65

ASIAN CHEESECAKE

SERVINGS: 4 servings

COOKING TIME: 90 minutes

Ingredients:
2 eggs
40 g sugar
20 g butter
60 ml 3.2% or 4% milk
100 g ricotta cheese
40 g wheat flour type 500
10 g potato flour

INSTRUCTIONS:

Melt the butter in a bowl and add the cheese and pour in the milk, stirring all the time.
Let the resulting mixture cool, then add egg yolks and sifted flour.
Beat egg whites to stiff foam , then add a pinch of salt and then gradually add sugar.
Then beat the egg whites with sugar to a smooth foam.Combine the egg whites with the cheese mixture, mix thoroughly.
Line a baking tray with baking paper, pour in the cake mixture.
Wrap the tin from the outside with aluminum foil.Transfer the prepared cake into a larger tin and fill it with water.Put the cake with the extra tin into the oven and bake for 15 minutes at 400 F, and then for 30 minutes at 275 F.

Energy per serving : 100 g
calorie count 215 kcal
Protein 7 g
Carbohydrates 22 g
Glycemic index 85

SUMMARY TIPS AND CONCLUSION

The Mediterranean diet for a healthy heart and body carries a number of beneficial health effects. The most important of these is weight reduction. Weight loss usually results from an energy deficit.
Good weight reduction on the Mediterranean diet is further supported by huge amounts of very good for the body nutrients, minerals, vitamins, fiber. Thus, this diet counteracts cardiovascular disease and thanks to it you can improve the results of the lipidogram.
The right products that are sources of unsaturated fatty acids reduce the proportion of unfavorable cholesterol and increase the proportion of favorable cholesterol.

In addition to these effects, the brain and immune system will also be strengthened. Unsaturated fatty acids have anti-inflammatory effects. What's more, this diet can have a significant impact on cancer prevention. Following a Mediterranean diet also has an impact on preventing the development of Alzheimer's disease and other civilization diseases of this age.
The most important principles that help in this direction are, first of all, taking pleasure in your meals, but also in your own life. Stress is not conducive to health.
An important point is to eat products that come from your own neighborhood. The idea is to consume processed products as little as possible.
The focus should be on self-prepared meals. Mediterranean cuisine is based primarily on local products that Italy, Spain and Greece, among others, are famous for - olives, fish, seafood and others.
It is also important that the products on the menu are selected seasonally.
The Mediterranean diet is based primarily on healthy sources of fats and herbs, not forgetting proteins and carbohydrates.
And importantly, wine is drunk with the meal, dry wine of course, in the amount of one or two glasses for lunch or dinner.

21 DAYS MEAL PLAN

1 week

	Breakfast	Lunch	Dinner	Desserts
1	SCRAMBLED EGGS IN OLIVE OIL WITH SUN-DRIED TOMATOES	ROASTED ZUCCHINI WITH SPICES	MEDITERRANEAN CLASSIC SALAD	CHOCOLATE TART WITH STRAWBERRIES
2	TOASTED BREAD WITH MOZZARELLA AND MUSHROOMS	CREAM SOUP WITH RUTABAGAS AND CARROTS	LECHO WITH MUSHROOMS AND ZUCCHINI	DESSERT COTTA WITH STRAWBERRIES AND RASPBERRIES
3	PUMPKIN PIES	PEPERONATA WITH HERBS	BAKED SALMON	COCKTAIL WITH KALE AND FRUIT
4	SANDWICH WITH HUMMUS,PICKLED CUCUMBER AND TURKEY	SPAGHETTI CARBONARA WITH HERBS	BAKED APPLES	BLUEBERRY MUFFINS
5	SALAD OF FRESH SEASONAL FRUITS AND LEAFY GREENS AND CHEESE	VEGETABLE STEW CAPONATA	POLENTA FRIES	PUMPKIN AND SUNFLOWER CAKE
6	BARLEY GROATS WITH BANANA AND STRAWBERRIES	RED BEAN CUTLETS WITH SOY SAUCE	RICE WITH SPINACH	DESSERT OF STRAWBERRIES AND MASCARPONE
7	OATMEAL WITH RAISINS, NUTS AND APPLE	PIZZA WITH SHRIMP AND HERBS	PUMPKIN RISOTTO WITH SPICES	GRILLED VEGETABLE SKEWERS

21 DAYS MEAL PLAN

2 week

	Breakfast	Lunch	Dinner	Desserts
1	MACKEREL OR TUNA PASTE FOR SANDWICHES	TOFU WITH VEGETABLES	CHICKPEAS IN TOMATO SAUCE	DESSERT WITH WATERMELON
2	PANCAKES WITH RICOTTA AND APPLES	CAULIFLOWER SOUP WITH ONIONS	TROUT FILLET WITH LEEK AND MARJORAM	FRIED BANANAS
3	STUFFED CHERRY TOMATOES WITH COTTAGE CHEESE	ROASTED KOHLRABI WITH TOMATO SAUCE	PASTA WITH BRAISED FENNEL AND ARUGULA	OATCAKES
4	SCRAMBLED EGGS WITH GREEN BEANS AND CHIVES	BOTWINA COOLER SOUP	PANCAKES WITH KIMCHI AND MAPLE SYRUP	TART WITH CHERRIES
5	BAKED BUNS WITH VEGETABLES AND EGG	PASTA CASSEROLE WITH CHICKEN AND VEGETABLES	KHACHAPURI WITH EGG AND SPICES	FLOURLESS PANCAKES WITH MAPLE SYRUP
6	CARROT BANANA AND STRAWBERRY PANCAKES	STEAMED FISH	SHRIMP IN CREAM SAUCE AND HERBS	RASPBERRY JAM
7	WHOLE WHEAT BREAD WITH SALMON AND OLIVES	CHICKEN WITH SPINACH	BRAISED MUSSELS	SUGAR-FREE BROWNIE

21 DAYS MEAL PLAN

3 week

	Breakfast	Lunch	Dinner	Desserts
1	COCONUT PANCAKES WITH RASPBERRIES	PASTA WITH SPINACH AND SALMON	FOCACCIA WITH SUN-DRIED TOMATOES AND OLIVES	CHOCOLATE MOUSSE
2	YOGURT WITH TANGERINE, BLUEBERRIES AND NUTS	LIGHT BEET SOUP	GREEK-STYLE STUFFED ZUCCHINI	VANILLA PUDDING WITH BANANA
3	SCHICKEN MOZZARELLA AND TOMATO SALAD	VEGETABLE PANCAKESE	PASTA WITH NUTS AND CREAM SAUCE	BUCKWHEAT WITH COTTAGE CHEESE AND FRUIT
4	SCRAMBLED EGGS WITH ASPARAGUS	PUMPKIN SALAD	OMELETTE WITH AVOCADO	COUNTRY CHEESE AND RAISIN PANCAKES
5	PANCAKES WITH CHEESE	SHRIMP IN BUTTER WITH GARLIC AND THYME	KHACHAPURI WITH EGG AND SPICES	TART WITH OREO AND CREAM
6	BANANA IN BATTER	BUCKWHEAT GROATS WITH EGG	PASTA SALAD WITH SALAMI AND SPICES	ZEPPOLE DOUGHNUTS WITH CREAM
7	TROUT PASTE SANDWICHES	SALAD WITH CRANBERRIES	PASTA CASSEROLE WITH CHICKEN	ASIAN CHEESECAKE

SHOPPING LIST OF HEALTHY PRODUCTS FROM THE MEDITERRANEAN DIET

VEGETABLES:

Beets, savoy cabbage , eggplant, leek, parsley, asparagus, artichokes, potatoes, garlic, broccoli, Brussels sprouts, zucchini yams, pumpkin, radicchio, fennel, lettuces, red, green, yellow peppers, tomatoes, onions, capers, olives.

FRUITS:

Avocados, strawberries, oranges, apples, tangerines, lemon, pomegranate, apricots, cherries, peaches, figs, dates, melon.

FISH AND SEAFOOD:

Trout, salmon, mackerel, tuna, sardines, herring, cod, squid, shrimp, octopus, oysters, moules.

LEGUMES:

Peas, beans, lentils, chickpeas.

CEREAL PRODUCTS:

Buckwheat, barley, millet, quinoa, amaranth, bulgur groats, wild rice, brown rice,rye bread.

FATS OILS:

Olive oil or cold-pressed canola oil.

NUTS AND SEEDS:

Walnuts, almonds, cashews, pistachios, pine nuts, sesame seeds, pumpkin seeds, cumin seeds, sunflower seeds, chia seeds, flaxseeds.

DAIRY PRODUCTS:

mozzarella, twaróg, ser feta, parmezan, ricotta, jogurt, kefir, maślanka, halloumi.

SPICES AND HERBS:

Thyme, basil, rosemary, marjoram, coriander, bay leaf, turmeric, parsley, allspice, paprika, thyme, Roman cumin, cinnamon, tarragon, cloves, mint, dill, sage.